CREWEL EMBROIDERY

CREWEL EMBROIDERY

A Practical Guide

SHELAGH AMOR

Sally Milner Publishing

First published in 2002 by
Sally Milner Publishing Pty Ltd
PO Box 2104
Bowral NSW 2576
AUSTRALIA

© Shelagh Amor 2002

Design by Anna Warren, Warren Ventures Pty Ltd
Stitch diagrams by Anna Warren, Warren Ventures Pty Ltd
Edited by Anne Savage
Photography by Sergio Santos

Printed in China

National Library of Australia Cataloguing-in-Publication data:
Amor, Shelagh.
    Crewel embroidery.

    ISBN 1 86351 298 5.

    1. Crewelwork. I. Title. (Series : Milner craft series).

    746.446

10 9 8 7 6 5 4 3 2 1

CONTENTS

Introduction	6
Historical notes	7
Materials and tools	9
Transferring designs	12
Framing up	15
Colour principles	19
Colour choices for crewel embroidery	24
Starting to embroider	26
Crewel designs and stitches	**28**
Design no. 1	29
Design no. 2	33
Design no. 3	36
Design no. 4	40
Design no. 5	44
Design no. 6	48
Design no. 7	52
Design no. 8	56
Design no. 9	60
Creating a Tree of Life design	**64**
Design no. 10	68
Creating a scroll design	**73**
Design no. 11	78
Blocking	84
Design sheets	86
Stitch glossary	93
About the author	111
Acknowledgements	112

INTRODUCTION

This book came into being in part as a result of the many embroidery classes I have conducted, and in part from my awareness that many embroiderers like to have a manual for help and guidance after their classes have come to an end. With this in mind, my aim in presenting it is to give confidence to the novice embroiderer and to provide a design source for the more experienced.

As with all embroidery techniques, the working of crewel embroidery is meant to be an enjoyable pursuit. This style of embroidery is adaptable to a wide range of purposes, including fashion items, soft furnishings and wall hangings. The satisfaction derived from creating these items yourself will give pleasure for many years.

Crewel embroidery is a form of embroidery based on surface stitches, many of which will already be familiar to some embroiderers. This book demonstrates how these stitches are used in crewel work and explains basic rules which will help any embroiderer to achieve the best results.

While there are more than one hundred stitches and variations which may be used in crewel embroidery, it is not necessary to use all of them—or even to be able to work them. Indeed, an embroiderer with a very small repertoire of stitches may produce a beautiful piece of crewel work. Far more important is the way the stitches are used, and the choice of colour and design, which can combine to create an exciting piece of work.

The beginner to crewel work might like to begin with five or six stitches—say stem, chain and split stitches, long and short stitch, French knots and perhaps a simple trellis filling—which form a good basis for crewel embroidery. Once these stitches have been mastered, more stitches may readily be added to your repertoire.

This book will give guidance to the novice embroiderer who wishes to embark on crewel work and will enable the more experienced embroiderer to acquire greater skill and derive more enjoyment through exploring the technique further.

HISTORICAL NOTES

Crewel embroidery is a form of needlework stitched in a two-ply worsted yarn known as crewel wool—which gives the technique its name. Although, strictly speaking, any embroidery worked in crewel wool may be considered crewel work, the term has come to mean a particular style of embroidery with bold and fanciful designs which started to evolve during the sixteenth century and reached its height during the seventeenth century.

The designs came from nature and encompassed trees and flowers, animals and insects, sometimes realistic in form and at other times quite fantastic. From an embroiderer's point of view, it is this degree of freedom of form that gives crewel embroidery its charm. Since there are no rules or boundaries to the way a flower or a tree may be executed, crewel embroiderers are limited only by their imagination.

Wool embroidery has been worked in many countries from very early times, although all too few of the early pieces remain today. Perhaps the best-known piece of wool embroidery is the Bayeux Tapestry—which is not a tapestry at all—telling the tale of the Norman conquest of England. It is embroidered in worsted wool in browns, reds, indigos and golds on a linen ground 70 metres long but only 50 centimetres wide.

Crewel work as we know it today developed during the seventeenth century, at a time when there was a brisk trade between Europe and the Far East. The ships of the East India Company carried painted cotton hangings, or palampores, to England. The designs on the hangings were of the Tree of Life rising from decorative mounds, with fanciful flowers and leaves and small animals in the foreground. These designs became popular with English embroiderers and so emerged a style of needlework that featured a variety of fruits and flowers all springing from the same plant with a complete disregard for realism. Embroiderers are indebted to that period in history which gave birth to a form of needlework that remains popular to this day. Technically this style of embroidery should be called Jacobean work. While Jacobean work is crewel work, not all crewel work is Jacobean in style.

During the eighteenth century these European fashions flowed on to the New World and the colonial housewife, like her English counterpart, embroidered bed hangings, covers and pillows in crewel designs, having first woven her own linen and spun and dyed her own yarn. Probably because of the difficulties of home dyeing, a great deal of American crewel work was embroidered in blue and white, and stitches tended to be those where most of the thread was on the top of the fabric.

The shapes that had their origins in the seventeenth and eighteenth centuries have continued to influence crewel embroidery into the twenty-first century. While we no longer use bed hangings, crewel work can be used to enhance practically any other item which lends itself to embroidered decoration.

MATERIALS AND TOOLS

Fabrics

Traditionally, crewel embroidery was worked on a strong natural-coloured linen or linen and cotton twill fabric. This same twill is still a good choice today but, as it has become expensive and may not be available everywhere, it is worth experimenting with a selection of fabrics to find others which suit the task. To avoid waste of time and materials, choose a fabric which is sufficiently strong and closely woven to support the variety of stitches which will be worked. If you would like to use a fabric which is not strong enough for the purpose, a backing of closely woven preshrunk cotton should be used with it. The two fabrics are worked as one to produce the required strength.

Furnishing fabrics and dress fabrics constructed from linen, cotton, wool or a mixture of any of these yarns are worth experimenting with, provided they are strong and closely woven. Always stitch a sample piece before embarking on a major project. It is disappointing to get halfway through a piece of embroidery only to find that the ground fabric is proving less than ideal.

When calculating the amount of fabric you need to purchase for any embroidery project, it is always good policy to allow an extra amount which may be used for experimenting with colours and stitches as the work progresses, or even for checking stitch tension when picking up the work after a lapse of some time.

Always remove any creases from your fabric before applying the design.

Yarns

A fine two-ply wool yarn is the traditional working thread for crewel embroidery. Appleton of England manufactures crewel wool in a wide range of colours, with as many as nine values of some colours. Because crewel wool is so fine, the embroiderer may work with more than one thread in the needle, depending on the scale of the work.

Purists may say that only crewel wools should be used in crewel embroidery but many others say that cottons or silks may be used as highlighters. The choice is in your hands.

To allow scope for introducing shading into your embroidery it is worth buying from three to five values of your chosen colours. These may be consecutive values or values spaced over the range available. Store the tags bearing the colour codes with a small sample of the wool. You will almost certainly need to refer to them when re-ordering.

Crewel embroidery was first worked in wool on linen because those were the materials most readily available—some early workers would have needed to spin and weave their own linen from flax, and to spin and dye their own wools. Today, linen twill is still a good choice for a background fabric, with modern fabrics expanding the embroiderer's choice. Many embroidery threads are now available to supplement the wool—cotton pearl, stranded cotton, soft embroidery cotton, silk, rayon, metal thread.

Needles

Crewel needles with sharp points and oval eyes are most commonly used for crewel embroidery. As a general guide, size 3 is suitable for working two strands of wool, and size 4 for one strand. Where a cotton or silk thread is being used, smaller sizes of needle will probably be more suitable, depending on the thickness of the thread. If a shorter needle is preferred a chenille needle, size 23, may suit the task.

Tapestry needles are used for darning stitches, where a sharp point might split the wool.

Magnifying glass

Many embroiderers find it necessary to use a magnifying glass. A word of warning here—when working under a magnifying glass it is hard to determine the true length of the stitches and many people have a tendency to make their stitches too short. Be sure to establish the correct length of the stitches before you bring the magnifier into use.

Embroidery frames

Some stitches may be worked without using an embroidery frame, but many stitches can only be executed successfully with the fabric stretched tightly in a frame. Stitches such as satin stitch, long and short stitch, laid stitch and squared fillings are so characteristic of crewel work that to leave them out for lack of a frame would severely limit the scope of your embroidery. It is therefore important to become accustomed to using a frame from the outset. A circular frame with a diameter of 14–20 cm (5½–8 inches) is suggested for samplers. The smaller size is easier to work with.

All the examples illustrated in this book, with the exception of the scroll design on page 73, were worked in a circular frame with an inner diameter of 15 cm (6 inches). The frame was moved as necessary with no injury to the stitches already worked. The scroll design was worked in a rectangular frame.

TRANSFERRING DESIGNS

There are several methods of transferring a design to fabric. It is advisable to do a test run on a corner of your fabric before transferring a whole design, since not all methods suit all fabrics.

Water-erasable pen

The advent of the water-erasable pen has made the transferring of embroidery designs much easier than in the past. The design is first traced onto tracing paper with a black felt pen and the tracing then secured to a light box with masking tape. The fabric is centred over the tracing and this too is secured with masking tape. It is now quite a simple task to trace the design onto the fabric using a fine water-erasable pen.

Because the markings are not permanent, a line may be removed and inserted elsewhere. A line that is not completely covered with embroidery may also be removed when the embroidery is completed, provided the fabric has not been pressed. Remember that the heat of an iron may permanently set the markings.

If a light box is not available, a brightly lit window will serve the same purpose.

Advantages Quick and easy to use.
Disadvantages In some instances lines which have been removed can reappear.

Tacking

In this method the design is traced onto tissue paper which is then pinned in position on the fabric. Using a small running stitch through paper and fabric, the design is stitched onto the fabric. The tissue paper is then gently torn away.

Advantages Lines may be altered as required.
Disadvantages This method is more time consuming and laborious than most of the other methods.

Embroidery transfer

An embroidery transfer is placed shiny side down on the fabric and pinned securely. The back of the design is pressed with a fairly hot iron, using an up and down movement rather than a smoothing action, to avoid smudging the lines. Any manufacturer's instructions on the transfer must be cut away first; these may be used to test for the required heat and the necessary pressure to transfer the design to the fabric.

Advantages Quick to apply.
Disadvantages Once applied, the lines are permanent, so they must be covered with embroidery. Embroidery transfers do not always work well on textured fabrics.

Transfer pencil

Using a transfer pencil, the design is traced onto tracing paper and the tracing then used in the same way as any purchased embroidery transfer, that is, placed face down on the fabric and pressed with a hot iron.

The transfer pencil must be kept sharp to give as fine a line as possible. A thick or blurry line may prove difficult to cover. It is important to experiment with a small shape to find the degree of pressure required on the transfer pencil to give a clear line when transferred.

Remember that the design will be reversed when using this method— you may prefer to make your tracing from the back of the design.

Advantages Quick to use once the tracing is made.
Disadvantages As with embroidery transfers the lines are permanent and must be covered with embroidery. Some transfer pencils may 'bleed' into the fabric.

Dressmaker's carbon

Dressmaker's carbon may be purchased from fabric stores. A sheet of it is placed face down between the design and the fabric and the three layers weighted down at the corners to prevent movement. The lines of the design are then traced very firmly so that the design is imprinted on the fabric. A fine steel knitting needle is a suitable implement for the purpose.

Advantages This method is more suited to smooth fabrics.
Disadvantages Lines are permanent and must be covered with embroidery. This method may not be suited to textured fabrics.

Prick and pounce

The design is first traced off onto a firm tracing paper. The tracing paper is then laid on a soft pad such as an ironing pad, a thick layer of felt, a folded blanket or similar, and the lines of the design pricked at close intervals. The pricked tracing is laid on top of the framed fabric and weighted down at the corners.

Roll a strip of felt approximately 5 cm wide and 15 cm long (2 inches by 6 inches) and stitch the ends to secure them to make a felt pounce pad. Dip the end of the felt pad into powdered charcoal or chalk and rub over the lines of the design, using a light pressure and a circular motion. The pounce powder will be forced through the holes in the design onto the fabric. Before removing the pricked design, lift a corner to check that the design is showing clearly on the fabric. Once you are sure that the design is sufficiently clear, lift the pricking off the fabric and store it for future use.

Using a fine brush and blue watercolour paint, join the dots. Add sufficient water to make the paint flow evenly, but do not thin it too much or it will bleed into the fabric.

When the paint is quite dry any remaining pounce powder may be shaken from the fabric.

Advantages The tracing may be used a number of times.
Disadvantages This method may be a little time consuming.

FRAMING UP

Circular frames

To prepare a circular frame for use the inner ring is bound with tape. Bias binding, opened out to its full width, will serve the purpose. The bias binding is bound over and over the ring, each layer slightly overlapping the previous one. When the ring is completely covered, the bias tape is cut and the end turned under and stitched down to secure. This binding will help to prevent the fabric from slipping in the frame.

The following illustration shows the two parts of a circular frame with the inner ring bound with tape.

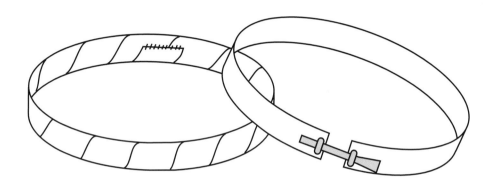

To mount the fabric in the frame, place the inner ring on a flat surface and lay the embroidery fabric over it so that the part of the design to be worked is centred over the ring. Adjust the screw on the outer ring so that it will fit snugly over fabric and inner ring. Place the outer ring in position over the fabric and press halfway home; pull the fabric taut, making sure that the grain of the fabric is straight in both directions, then press the outer ring all the way home.

To release the frame simply press down on the inner ring with both thumbs.

Square or rectangular frames

Method 1
1. Mark the midpoints of the webbing on the top and bottom rollers.
2. Mark the midpoints of the top and bottom edges of the fabric.

3. Machine stitch a piece of webbing down each side of the fabric or tack in position by hand using a horizontal tacking stitch. The webbing should measure 5 cm (2 inches) in width and be the same weight as the fabric.

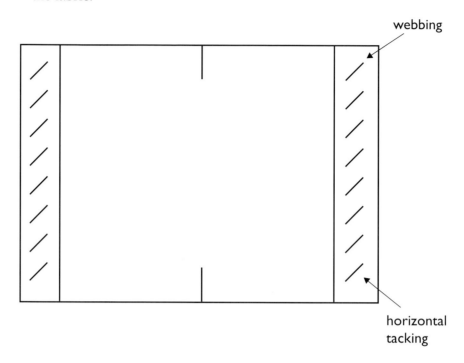

webbing

horizontal
tacking

4. Turn over about 12 mm (½ inch) along the top and bottom edges of the fabric. Match the midpoint of one edge of the fabric with the midpoint of the webbing on one of the rollers. Beginning with a knot and a double stitch, oversew the webbing and the fabric together, working from the centre outwards. End by stitching back over the last three or four stitches, forming cross-stitches. Return to the centre and stitch in the opposite direction. Stitch the fabric to the opposite roller in the same way.

5. Assemble the frame and lace the sides of the fabric to the side timbers of the frame with strong string, stitching about 12 mm (½ inch) into the webbing. Leave about 50 cm (20 inches) of string free at the top and bottom of the frame for securing.

6. Wrap the surplus strings at the top of the frame around the corner joints and secure firmly with a slip knot. Tighten the strings evenly down each side, making sure that the grains of the fabric remain straight. Wrap any surplus string around the bottom corners of the frame and secure as the top corners.

At this point the fabric will be drum tight and ready for use. Should the fabric in the frame become slack as the embroidery progresses, tighten the strings at the sides as necessary.

Method 2

1. Mark the midpoints of the webbing on the top and bottom rollers.
2. Mark the midpoints of the top and bottom edges of the fabric.
3. Form a piping down the sides of the fabric by turning over about 2 cm (¾ inch) of fabric while inserting a length of piping cord or strong string that has been knotted at each end. Stitch the piping in place by machine, or by hand using a backstitch.

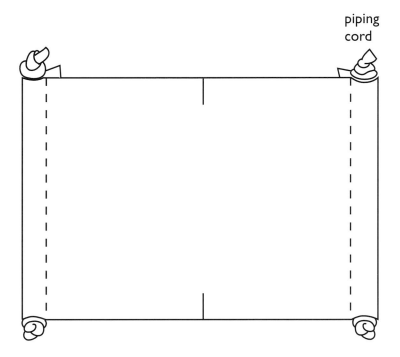

piping cord

4. Turn over about 12 mm (½ inch) along the top and bottom edges of the fabric. Match the midpoint of the top of the fabric with the midpoint of the webbing on the top roller and, beginning with a knot and a double stitch, oversew the tape and the fabric together, working from the centre outwards. End by stitching back over the last three or four stitches, forming cross-stitches. Return to the centre and stitch towards the opposite side.
Stitch the bottom of the fabric to the webbing on the bottom roller in the same way.
5. Assemble the frame and, using a strong string, lace the sides of the fabric to the side timbers of the frame, stitching into the casings so that the stitches take in the piping on each side. Leave about 50 cm (20 inches) of string free at the start and finish of the lacing.
6. Wrap the surplus strings at the top of the frame around the corner joints and secure firmly with a slip knot. Tighten the strings evenly down each side, making sure that the grains of the fabric remain

straight. Wrap any surplus string around the bottom corners of the frame and secure as the top corners.

At this point the fabric will be very taut and ready for use. Should the fabric in the frame become slack as the work progresses, tighten the strings at the sides as necessary.

The illustration below shows fabric mounted in a square frame with Method 1 used on the left-hand side and Method 2 used on the right-hand side.

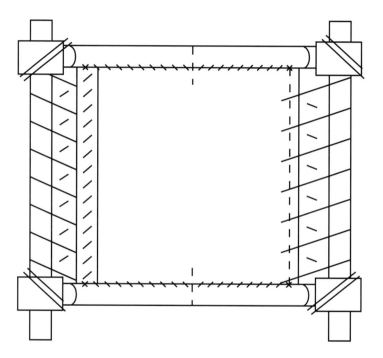

COLOUR PRINCIPLES

Once you have decided on a design, the next important decision to be made is the colours to use for your embroidery. This can be a difficult step because embroidery threads come in such a wide range of colours. The choice is further complicated by the number of tints and shades which are produced in each colour. To stand in front of the display board of any single manufacturer of embroidery threads and attempt to make a selection for a forthcoming project confronts the average embroiderer with a task which may take some considerable time. A few basic principles, therefore, will help to make the task a little easier.

The colour wheel

Primary colours
Beginning with a circle, the three primary colours—red, blue and yellow— are placed at equidistant points around the edge of the circle. If you imagine a clock face, yellow will be placed at number 12, red at number 4 and blue at number 8.

Secondary colours
When two primary colours are mixed, a secondary colour is produced. Yellow and blue give us green at number 10 on the clock face, red and yellow produce orange at number 2 and red and blue make violet at number 6.

Tertiary colours
A tertiary colour is produced when a primary colour is mixed with an adjacent secondary colour to produce yellow/orange and yellow/green, blue/green and blue/violet, red/orange and red/violet. Note that the name of the primary colour is placed before the name of the secondary colour.

Hue Hue refers to the name of a colour, e.g. red, green, yellow, etc.
Tint Any colour or hue with the addition of white.
Shade Any colour or hue with the addition of black.
Value Tints and shades are values of a hue or colour
Intensity or chroma These words are used to describe the brightness or

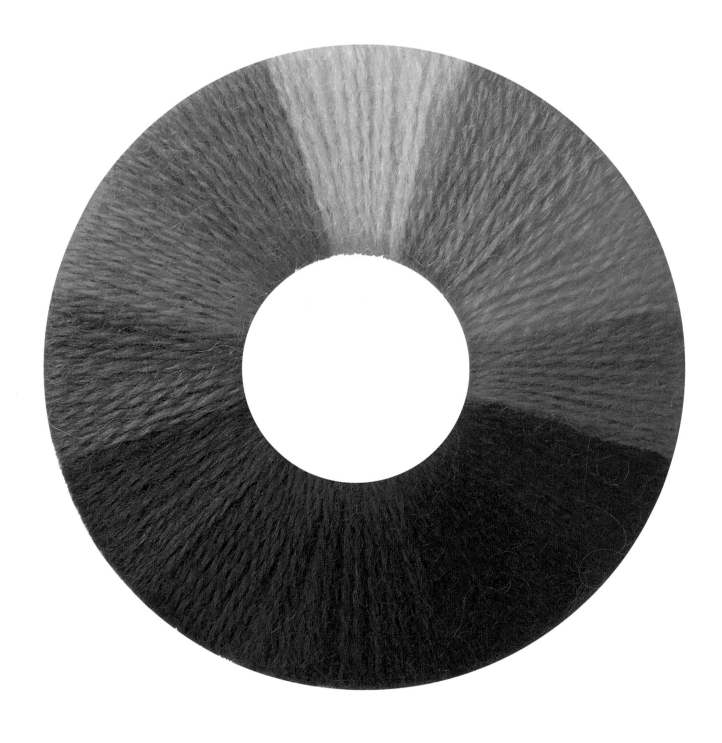

dullness of a colour. Adding grey to a pure colour causes it to lose its brightness or chroma. The more grey that is added, the duller the colour becomes. Adding grey to pure colours creates tones.

Looking at colours in their pure form, yellow is always the lightest colour on the colour wheel and violet the darkest. By placing yellow at number 12 on a clock face, whichever way you travel around the clock the colours will get darker until you reach violet at number 6.

Colour schemes

The positioning of the colours around the colour wheel forms the basis for selecting an appropriate colour scheme.

Complementary scheme
Complementary colours are those which lie directly opposite each other on the colour wheel—for example, red and green, yellow and violet, blue and orange are all complementary colours. When complementary colours are used together, they will always appear at their brightest.

Split complementary scheme
Split complementary schemes are those where a colour from one side of the wheel is used with the colour on each side of its complementary colour. For example, the complementary colour of red is green but the split complementary colours of red are yellow/green and blue/green.

Triadic scheme
A triadic scheme is made up of three colours placed at equal distances round the colour wheel—for example, the three primaries, red, blue and yellow; the three secondary colours, green, violet and orange; or a group of three tertiary colours, such as orange/yellow, blue/green and red/violet, or yellow/green, blue/violet and red/orange.

Analogous scheme
Analogous colours are those which are adjacent on the colour wheel—up to five adjoining segments. Such a scheme might contain green, blue/green, blue, blue/violet and violet. A bit of zing may be provided by adding a little of the complementary of the central of the five colours. In this example the complementary would be orange.

Monochromatic scheme

The use of one colour only, with its tints and shades, is called a monochromatic scheme.

Warm colours

Reds, oranges and yellows are classed as warm colours. They are bright and happy colours which appear to come forward and draw attention to themselves.

Cool colours

The cool colours are blues, greens and blue/violets. They seem to recede into the background.

Neutral colours

These are the browns and greys. Browns fall in the low intensity ranges in the yellow, orange and red portion of the colour wheel. Adding white to a brown shade gives beiges and tans. Greys are the values between black and white.

Sources of inspiration

If the use of the colour wheel seems all too technical, don't despair. Select an item whose colours you admire and which has at least three main colours, excluding white and black. It may be a painting, a fabric, a rug or an ornament. Take the quietest colour for the dominant colour in your embroidery, choose a brighter colour as your main accent colour and the brightest colour for a smaller accent.

Many artists advocate the use of a touch of yellow to add a dash of spice to a painting. This advice might also be used in embroidery.

For inspiration, look at colour schemes which come together in nature, such as the colours of flower species, the plumage of birds, the colours in a tree trunk. Use your imagination and you will come up with many sources of inspiration.

Examine the colours of mellowed brick, old fence palings and rock faces.

Fabrics and paintings are good sources of inspiration. These have often been created by colour experts and you will find them hard to beat.

Start a folio of magazine cuttings, wallpaper and fabric samples which you find pleasing. Before going to purchase your threads, have some idea of the basic colour or colours you would like to use. If necessary, take a sample from your folio with you. This will give you a starting point when confronted with the very wide selection available.

Colour combinations you admire may be captured on camera and stored for future reference.

Background fabric

In the way that the colour of your skin affects the colours you can wear, so too does your choice of background colour affect the colours that will look right in your finished embroidery. In the same way you need to take into account the timber of your furniture when selecting colours for seat covers, cushions and other soft furnishings.

Buying threads

Remember that you will not be using your chosen colours in equal quantities in your embroidery. Three or four single skeins of different colours will not give the same impression held in the hand as they will in your embroidery, where you might stitch 50 per cent of the total area in one colour and 10 per cent in another colour, with the other two colours covering the remaining 40 per cent of the area.

COLOUR CHOICES FOR CREWEL EMBROIDERY

Consider first the setting for your embroidery. If it is to hang on a wall, look at the colours which will surround it—carpet, curtains, walls, lampshades and any other appointments. If your embroidery will be made up into a handbag, consider the garments with which you would like to use it. Carrying out this exercise will immediately direct you towards certain colours. Remember that when selecting the number of colours to be used it is better to err on the side of restraint. Crewel work is not an exercise in using every colour on the palette but rather one of selecting a few colours which will produce a beautiful result.

Traditional crewel embroidery was worked predominantly in green, with the secondary colours being blue and a rich chestnut-brown through to yellow. They were not used in a naturalistic way, with stems worked in brown, leaves in green and flowers in red and yellow. Instead the colours were used in a random fashion, in whatever combination the embroiderer saw fit. Because the threads were home-dyed, these colours were muted. For the beginner, muted colours are still a good choice. Note that muted does not mean pale but rather the opposite of bright. With experience, more adventurous schemes may be chosen.

Crewel embroidery may be worked in a monochromatic scheme with variations of one colour only. Early Jacobean embroidery was worked in this way. Much early American crewel embroidery was worked in blue, which was easily obtained from the indigo plant. It was this early colonial style of work which a group of women in Deerfield, Massachusetts revived in the late nineteenth century, along with other earlier arts. The fact that only one colour was used never led to the work being uninteresting.

Two colours may be chosen and a range of each of those colours used to very good effect. For example, you could work in a selection of reds and greens, each in three or four values.

The adventurous embroiderer may like to use several different colours in a single piece of work, in which case it is important to aim for a balanced effect. A good rule of thumb to follow is the triangle pattern, where patches of the same colour are arranged in three different areas of the design.

Before starting your embroidery decide where the light source will be. Right-handed people usually work with the light coming from their left, while left-handed embroiderers tend to prefer the light on their right. With this in mind it will be easy to decide which areas will be light and which will be dark.

When shading a stem or a tree trunk, the lightest area will be to the front and slightly off-centre. When the light is coming from the left the lightest area will be to the left of centre; when the light is coming from the right the lightest area will be to the right of centre.

Armed with this information, the best way to learn about colour is to experiment.

STARTING TO EMBROIDER

Length of thread

In general, the maximum length of thread advisable is 40 cm (16 inches). In working long stitches, such as in laid work, a longer thread may be appropriate. Experience soon tells you the length of thread that is most appropriate for the stitch.

Threading the needle

Threading a needle with wool can cause some frustration for the beginner to crewel embroidery. However, it does become easier with practice.

Begin by looping the wool over the needle (diagram 1).

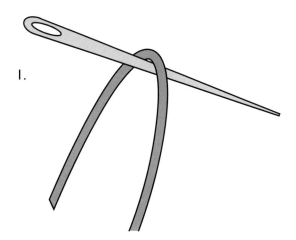

1.

Squeeze the loop and the needle between the thumb and first finger of the left hand, with the needle in a horizontal position (diagram 2).

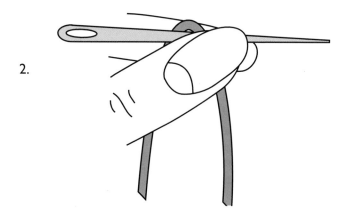

2.

Pull the needle out of the loop and, maintaining a tight hold on the loop, place the eye of the needle over the loop. Push the needle down while passing the loop of wool through the eye of the needle (diagram 3).

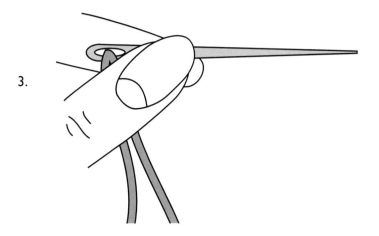

3.

Starting and finishing a thread

Starting

1. Take two or three small running stitches where they will be covered by the first few embroidery stitches. This gives a neat start on the front of the work and on the back.
2. Take two small back stitches where they will be covered by future stitching.

Finishing

1. Weave the tail through the back of the stitches already worked.
2. Take two small back stitches where they will be covered by subsequent stitching.
3. Take two tiny back stitches against the previously worked stitching line. Finish by bringing the thread through to the front of the work, placing some tension on the thread and cutting off the tail close to the fabric. The thread will sink below the surface of the fabric, leaving no visible trace.

   Make it a rule never to leave tails of thread hanging on the back of the work. Inevitably you will bring them through to the front as you stitch, making your embroidery look messy.

CREWEL DESIGNS AND STITCHES

This section contains a series of nine designs and shows the stitches which may be used to execute them.

The first design introduces the six stitches most commonly used in crewel embroidery. Additional stitches are introduced in later designs, allowing embroiderers to gain confidence and enjoyment as they progress through the nine projects.

Each of the designs has been stitched with Appleton crewel wool. Alternative crewel wools may be used and colours may be altered to suit the taste of the embroiderer.

DESIGN NO. 1

This first design introduces the six stitches which may be considered essential to all crewel embroidery. You will probably use some or all of these stitches in every piece of crewel embroidery which you work.

Stitch the areas at the back of the design first, then follow with the areas at the front.

Requirements

*Linen twill or firmly woven fabric of your choice,
    measuring 30 cm (12 inches) square*
Embroidery frame
Crewel needles:
    no. 3 for use with two threads
    no. 4 for use with a single thread
Appleton crewel wools (one skein each):
    peacock blue nos. 642, 643 and 646
    (or crewel wool of your choice)

Method of working

Begin by transferring the design to your fabric using one of the methods described in the section on transferring designs. Mount the fabric in your frame, making sure that it is very tight.

Work the embroidery in the order described below. Use a single thread unless the instructions indicate otherwise. Instructions for working the stitches will be found in the Stitch Glossary.

1. Main stem This is worked in five rows of stem stitch, beginning at the left-hand side. The first four rows are worked from the flowerhead to the base of the stem, with the thread held to the left of the stem. Work two rows in peacock blue no. 643, one row in peacock blue no. 642 and one row in peacock blue no. 643. Stitch the final row in peacock blue no. 643, working in the opposite direction, that is, from bottom to top, with the thread kept to the right of the stem. Changing direction when working the final row of stem stitch ensures that the working thread lies on the outside of the shape, resulting in a smooth line.

2. Upper right leaf Work this leaf and its stem in stem stitch. Work two rows of stem stitch in peacock blue no. 642. Beginning with the underside of the leaf, stitch around the leaf and down the stem. Note that only the first two rows are used to form the stem; thereafter the rows are worked within the leaf. The third row is worked in peacock blue no. 642. This is followed with three rows in peacock blue no. 643. The remaining space is stitched in peacock blue no. 646.

3. The flower The centre of the flower is worked in a squared filling in peacock blue no. 642, tied with cross-stitches in peacock blue no. 646. French knots are added in two threads of peacock blue no. 642. The upper edge of the shape is worked in chain stitch in two threads of peacock blue no. 642.

Work the upper left-hand petal with a filling of stem stitch in peacock blue no. 643 and detached chain in peacock blue no. 646. The outline of this shape is worked in chain stitch in peacock blue no. 643.

The two lower petals of the flower are worked in long and short stitch over a row of split stitch in peacock blue nos. 642, 643 and 646.

4. Lower left leaf Work the leaf in long and short stitch over split stitch in peacock blue nos. 642, 643 and 646. The stem of this leaf is worked in stem stitch in two threads of peacock blue no. 643. The stem forms the vein of the leaf.

5. Large leaf This leaf is worked in a squared filling placed on the diagonal in peacock blue no. 642, tied with a straight stitch in peacock blue no. 643. The French knots are worked in two threads of peacock blue no. 646. The outline of the leaf is worked in two rows of stem stitch, with peacock blue no. 642 on the outside and peacock blue no. 643 on the inside.

The embroidery is now ready for blocking, as described on page 84, and may be made up as desired.

DESIGN NO. 2

This is another small design intended to give practice to the newcomer to crewel work. Two colours are used in this piece, showing how colour might be distributed for a balanced effect. However, the design might equally well be worked in three values of one colour.

As usual the areas at the back of the design are worked first, followed by the areas at the front.

Requirements

Linen twill or firmly woven fabric of your choice,
*   measuring 25 cm (10 inches) square*
Embroidery frame
Crewel needle no. 4
Appleton crewel wools (one skein each):
*   grey-green nos. 352, 353 and 355*
*   coral nos. 861, 863 and 864*
*   (or crewel wool of your choice)*

Method of working

Transfer the design to your fabric by using one of the methods described in the section on transferring designs on page 12. Mount the fabric in your frame, making sure that it is very tight.

Work the embroidery in the order described below. Use a single thread throughout. Instructions for working the stitches will be found in the Stitch Glossary.

1. Stem   Work the stem in stem stitch in grey-green no. 355 on the outsides and grey-green no. 353 in the centre. As with design no. 1, work the left-hand row and the centre row from top to bottom with the thread kept to the left, and the third row from bottom to top with the thread kept to the right.

2. Flower   Begin the centre petal of the flower by working three rows of chain stitch around the edge, using the three values of grey-green with the lightest on the outside and the darkest on the inside. The centre of this petal is worked in stem stitch in coral no. 864 and detached chain in coral no. 863.

The two outside petals are worked in long and short stitch over split stitch in the three values of coral.

3. Lower leaf   The lower leaf is also worked in long and short stitch over split stitch, using grey-green nos. 352 and 353 and coral no. 863.

The embroidery is now ready for blocking, as described on page 84, blocking and may be made up as desired.

DESIGN NO. 3

This design introduces two new stitches, satin stitch and closed fly stitch.

Requirements

Linen twill or fabric of your choice,
*   measuring approx. 30 x 24 cm (12 x 9.5 inches)*
Embroidery frame
Crewel needle no. 4
Appleton crewel wools (one skein each):
*   bright terra cotta nos. 221, 222, 223 and 224*
*   grass green nos. 252, 253 and 254*
*   grey-green nos. 352, 353, 354, 355, 356 and 357*
*   (or crewel wool of your choice)*

Method of working

Apply the design and mount the fabric in your frame, making sure that it is very tight.

Work with one thread in the needle throughout. Refer to the Stitch Glossary for stitch directions.

1. Stems Beginning with the main stem, work a row of stem stitch in grass green no. 253 and a row in grass green no. 254 between the main flower and the lower leaf. The side stems on the right and left are worked in grass green no.254.

2. Small leaves at the left These are worked in closed fly stitch in grass green no. 252.

3. Leaves below the main flower Work these leaves in long and short stitch over split stitch in grey-green nos. 352 and 353.

4. Main flower Begin at the centre of the flower with a simple squared filling worked in grass green no. 253 tied with bright terra cotta no. 224.

Then work the petals of the flower in long and short stitch over split stitch, completing the back petals first. Use bright terra cotta nos. 222 and 221 and grey-green no 352.

Now work the outline of the flower centre in chain stitch, using grey-green no. 354.

To finish this flower, work the front petals in long and short stitch over split stitch in bright terra cotta nos. 222, 223 and 224.

5. Small flower The centre of the small flower is worked in long and short stitch over split stitch in bright terra cotta nos. 221 and 222.

Work the outer petals in long and short stitch over split stitch in grey-green nos. 352 and 354.

The falling petals are worked in satin stitch over split stitch in bright terra cotta no. 224.

6. Large leaf This leaf is worked in long and short stitch over split stitch. Notice that both the greens are used in this leaf. The upper edge is worked in grass green no. 252 to resemble sunlight falling on the leaf, followed by grey-green no. 355 towards the centre. The lower edge of the leaf is worked in grey-green nos. 355, 356 and 357 at the centre, and the vein is worked in stem stitch in bright terra cotta no. 224.

The embroidery is now ready to be blocked and mounted as desired.

DESIGN NO.4

In Design no. 4 we meet three new stitches, coral stitch, battlemented couching and heavy chain stitch. Use a single thread in the needle unless directed otherwise.

Requirements

Linen twill or fabric of your choice,
 measuring approx. 35 x 28 cm (14 x 11 inches)
Embroidery frame
Crewel needles nos. 3 and 4
Tapestry needle no. 22
Appleton crewel wools (one skein each):
 wine red nos. 711, 712, 713, 714 and 715
 heraldic gold nos. 842 and 843
 gold no. 855
 grey-green nos. 354, 355, 356, 357 and 358
 (or crewel wool of your choice)

Method of working

Apply the design and mount the fabric in your frame, making sure that it is very tight.

Work with one thread in the needle, unless instructions indicate otherwise. Refer to the Stitch Glossary for stitch directions.

1. Stems The stems are worked in stem stitch as follows: work the main stem and the tendrils using two strands of grey-green nos. 354, 355 and 356. The finer stems bearing the small leaves on the right are worked in a single strand of grey-green no. 355.

2. Flower Begin at the centre, working the squared filling known as battlemented couching in heraldic gold nos. 842 and 843 and gold no. 855, tied down with grey-green no. 355. Finish this filling with French knots in two strands of wine red no. 714. The outer edge is worked in heavy chain stitch in two strands of grey-green no. 356 using a tapestry needle.

The upper middle petal is worked in long and short stitch over split stitch in grey-green nos. 354, 355, 356, 357 and 358.

The centres of the outer petals are worked in satin stitch over split stitch in wine red no. 711 and gold no. 855. Note that split stitch is not worked under the centre of the satin stitch. The petals are outlined in coral stitch in two strands of grey-green no. 355.

3. Group of three small leaves Each of these three leaves is worked in two detached chain stitches, one stitch inside the other, in grey-green no. 355 and heraldic gold no. 842.

4. Small leaves Work these leaves in long and short stitch over split stitch in grey-green nos. 354 and 355 and gold 855. The leaves are outlined in stem stitch in wine red no. 711.

5. Large leaf The outline of this leaf is worked in stem stitch in five tones each of grey-green nos. 354, 355, 356, 357 and 358 on the left-hand side and wine red nos. 711, 712, 713, 714 and 715 on the right-hand side. Work the French knot filling in two strands of heraldic gold no. 842.

The embroidery is now ready for blocking and making up.

DESIGN NO. 5

In this design we encounter two more stitches, buttonhole stitch and solid laid stitch, tied down with a contrasting squared filling anchored with straight stitches.

Requirements

Linen twill or fabric of your choice,
    measuring approx. 37 x 28 cm (14½ x 11 inches)
Embroidery frame
Crewel needles nos. 3 and 4
Tapestry needle no. 22
Appleton crewel wools (one skein each):
    Jacobean green nos. 291, 292, 293, 294, 295 and 297
    heraldic gold no. 844
    autumn yellow nos. 475 and 477
    (or crewel wools of your choice)

Method of working

Apply the design and mount the fabric in your frame, making sure that it is very tight.

Work with one thread in the needle, unless instructions indicate otherwise. Refer to the Stitch Glossary for stitch directions.

1. Leaf on left Begin with the squared filling in the centre of this leaf, using grey-green no. 291, tied with heraldic gold no. 844. Work the crosses in autumn yellow no. 475. Outline the leaf with three rows of chain stitch in Jacobean green nos. 293, 294 and 295. Work the centre vein in stem stitch, using Jacobean green no. 292. This vein extends into the stem.

2. Stems Complete the stems in stem stitch in Jacobean green nos. 292 and 293.

3. Main flower The centre of the main flower is worked in stem stitch and detached chain stitch in autumn yellow no. 475, with the outline worked in buttonhole stitch in heraldic gold no. 844.

The petal at centre left is worked in laid stitch in Jacobean green no. 294, overlaid with a trellis of heraldic gold no. 844 tied down with autumn yellow no. 477. Finally the petal is outlined with stem stitch in Jacobean green no. 294.

The two lower petals are outlined in three rows of stem stitch in Jacobean green, with the upper edges being worked in nos. 291, 292 and 293 and the lower edges in nos. 294, 295 and 297. The French knots are worked in two strands of Jacobean green no. 295.

4. Small flower Work the centre of this flower in stem stitch in Jacobean green no. 292 with detached chain stitches in heraldic gold no. 844, each enclosing a straight stitch in autumn yellow no. 475. The outline is heavy

chain stitch worked in two strands of Jacobean green no. 294, using a tapestry needle.

The outer petals are worked in long and short stitch over split stitch, using Jacobean green nos. 291, 292, 293 and 294.

5. Mounds Work the outside mounds in stem stitch in Jacobean green nos. 291 and 295. For the centre mound, use Jacobean green no. 295 and autumn yellow no. 477.

Work the tufts of grass in straight stitch in heraldic gold no. 844.

This design is now ready for blocking and making up as desired.

DESIGN NO. 6

T his design adds threaded herringbone stitch to the stitches met in earlier designs.

Requirements

Linen twill or fabric of your choice,
    measuring approx. 36 x 30 cm (14 x 12 inches)
Embroidery frame
Crewel needles nos. 3 and 4
Tapestry needle no. 22
Appleton crewel wools (one skein each):
    dull marine blue nos. 321, 322, 323 and 324
    bright terra cotta nos. 221, 222, 223 and 224
    gold no. 855
    heraldic gold nos. 841 and 843
    (or crewel wools of your choice)

Method of working

Apply the design and mount the fabric in your frame, making sure that it is very tight.

Work with one thread in the needle, unless instructions indicate otherwise. Refer to the Stitch Glossary for stitch directions.

1. Stems Begin at the top of the main stem, working in satin stitch in dull marine blue no. 323. Outline the satin stitch in stem stitch in dull marine blue nos. 322 and 323. The side stems are also worked in stem stitch, in dull marine blue nos. 322 and 323.

2. Upper right leaves The centres of these leaves are worked in herringbone stitch in dull marine blue no. 322 threaded with gold no. 855. Outline these leaves with a row of stem stitch in bright terra cotta no. 224.

3. Large flower The centre of the large flower is worked in long and short stitch over split stitch in bright terra cotta nos. 221, 222, 223 and 224.

The outer petals are worked in stem stitch and closed fly stitch in gold no. 855 and heraldic gold no. 843. The outline is heavy chain stitch in dull marine blue no. 323, worked with a tapestry needle.

4. Small flower Work the centre of the small flower in satin stitch in bright terra cotta nos. 221, 222, 223 and 224, commencing with the smallest round section and working a row of split stitch around that part of the shape that is not overlapped by the next section. Finish the main section of the flower with long and short stitch over split stitch in dull marine blue nos. 321, 322, 323 and 324.

5. Large leaf This leaf is worked in two parts, beginning with the upper side which is worked in threaded herringbone stitch in dull marine blue

no. 322 and gold no. 855. The vein of the leaf is worked in a row of stem stitch in dull marine blue no. 321 and the upper outline of the leaf is a row of stem stitch in dull marine blue no. 322. Work the lower outline of the leaf in stem stitch in three values of dull marine blue, starting on the outside with no. 323, followed by no. 322 and finally no. 321. To complete this leaf, work French knots inside the lower side of the leaf in heraldic gold no. 841 and gold no. 855, working with two strands in the needle.

6. Bottom leaf This leaf is worked in long and short stitch over split stitch. Work the underside of the leaf first in dull marine blue no. 324, followed by the main body of the leaf in dull marine blue nos. 321, 322 and 323.

The embroidery is now ready for blocking and making up.

DESIGN NO. 7

Design no. 7 adds seeding to those stitches encountered in earlier designs, and makes more extensive use of long and short stitch. The central leaf in this design has one edge turned so that we can see the underside. In embroidering the underside of a leaf or a petal, just as in embroidering the upper surface, care must be taken in angling the stitches correctly.

Requirements

Linen twill or firmly woven fabric of your choice,
*   measuring approx. 38 x 33 cm (15 x 13 inches)*
Embroidery frame
Crewel needle no. 4
Tapestry needle no. 22
Appleton crewel wools (one skein each):
*   Jacobean green nos. 291A, 291 and 292*
*   flame red nos. 203, 204, 205 and 206*
*   honeysuckle yellow nos. 692, 693 and 694*
*   grey-green nos. 351, 352, 353, 354 and 355*
*   (or crewel wools of your choice)*

Method of working

Apply the design and mount the fabric in your frame, making sure that it is very tight.

Work with one thread in the needle, unless instructions indicate otherwise. Refer to the Stitch Glossary for stitch directions.

1. **Stems** These are worked in stem stitch using Jacobean green nos. 291A and 292.

2. **Top flower** Begin with the leaf protruding beyond this flower, working in long and short stitch over split stitch using Jacobean green no. 292 and blending into grey-green nos. 354 and 355. The centre of the flower is worked in stem stitch and detached chain stitch in honeysuckle yellow no. 694 and outlined in coral stitch in flame red no. 206. The next two petals are worked in long and short stitch over split stitch in flame red nos. 204, 205 and 206. The remaining two petals are worked in long and short stitch over split stitch in grey-green nos. 353, 354 and 355.

3. Central leaf This leaf is worked in long and short stitch with the vein in stem stitch. Work the main part of the leaf, having first worked a row of split stitch around the right-hand side of the leaf, using grey-green nos. 352, 353, 354 and 355. The vein is worked in grey-green no. 355. Now work the upper part of the leaf in long and short stitch in Jacobean green nos. 291A and 292, with the vein in grey-green no. 355. The tendril is worked in stem stitch in Jacobean green 291A. Finally the curled-over side of the leaf is worked in satin stitch over split stitch in Jacobean green no. 291A, ensuring that the stitches lie in the right direction to create the curled-leaf effect.

4. Right-hand flower The petals of this flower are worked in chain stitch in honeysuckle yellow nos. 692, 693 and 694 and flame red no. 206, starting with the petal at the back, then working the middle petal and finally the front petal. The seeding is also worked in flame red no. 206. Finish the base of this flower in long and short stitch in Jacobean green no. 292 and grey-green no. 355.

5. Left-hand flower Work the centre of this flower in battlemented couching in honeysuckle yellow nos. 692, 693 and 694, tied down with flame red no. 206, and outlined with heavy chain stitch in Jacobean green no. 292, worked with a tapestry needle. The outer petals are worked in long and short stitch over split stitch in flame red nos. 203, 204, 205 and 206.

6. Small leaf at base This leaf is worked completely in chain stitch in Jacobean green nos. 291A and 292.

7. Large leaf at base Once again use long and short stitch over split stitch using grey-green nos. 351, 352 and 353, and Jacobean green no. 292.

The embroidery is now ready for blocking and making up.

DESIGN NO. 8

In this design we meet another squared filling, and laid stitches tied down with open fly stitch.

Requirements

Linen twill or fabric of your choice
    measuring approx. 30 x 28 cm (12 x 11 inches)
Embroidery frame
Crewel needles nos. 3 and 4
Tapestry needle no. 22
Appleton crewel wools (one skein each):
    flame red nos. 203, 204, 206 and 208
    mid blue nos. 151, 154 and 155
    (or crewel wools of your choice)

Method of working

Apply the design and mount the fabric in your frame, making sure that it is very tight.

Work with one thread in the needle, unless instructions indicate otherwise. Refer to the Stitch Glossary for stitch directions.

1. Large leaf In this design you begin with the leaves because they are behind the stem. The large leaf is worked in long and short stitch over split stitch in mid blue nos. 151, 154 and 155. The vein is worked in stem stitch in flame red nos. 204 and 206.

2. Small leaf Work the small leaf in satin stitch over an outline of split stitch in mid blue nos. 154 and 155. The vein is worked in stem stitch in flame red no. 206.

3. Stems The stems are worked in stem stitch in mid blue nos. 151, 154 and 155.

4. Main flower Begin with the centre of this flower, working a squared filling on the straight of the grain of the fabric, using flame red no. 206; over this work a squared filling on the cross grain, using mid blue no. 154. Tie down the diagonal filling with vertical straight stitches using flame red no. 208. Outline this filling in heavy chain stitch in two strands of mid blue no. 155, using a tapestry needle.

The centres of the next pair of petals are worked in long laid stitches in flame red no. 206, tied down with open fly stitch in mid blue no. 154 and outlined in stem stitch in flame red no. 206. The outer edge of these petals is worked in stem stitch in two strands of flame red no. 208.

The remaining three petals are worked in long and short stitch over split stitch in flame red nos. 203, 204, 206 and 208. The upper part of the petals is outlined in stem stitch in mid blue no. 154.

5. Small flower The petals are worked in long and short stitch over split stitch in flame red nos. 203, 204 and 206. The calyx is worked in French knots in two strands of mid blue no. 154.

6. Lower leaf This narrow leaf is worked in closed fly stitch in mid blue no. 154.

This design is now complete and ready for blocking and making up.

DESIGN NO. 9

In this design we introduce two animals. When embroidering animals, let the stitches follow the direction in which the fur or coat would normally grow. This isn't always easy when working in such confined spaces but keeping the colours simple will help.

Requirements

Linen twill or firmly woven fabric of your choice,
    measuring 28 x 30 cm (11 x 12 inches)
Embroidery frame
Crewel needles:
    no. 3 for use with two threads
    no. 4 for use with a single thread
Appleton crewel wools (one skein of each):
    peacock blue nos. 641, 642, 643 and 644
    biscuit brown nos. 761, 763, 764, 765 and 766
    (or crewel wools of your choice)

Method of working

Apply the design and mount the fabric in your frame, making sure that it is very tight.

Work with one thread in the needle, unless instructions indicate otherwise. Refer to the Stitch Glossary for stitch directions.

1. Uppermost leaf Begin this leaf with a squared filling worked on the diagonal in biscuit brown no. 766. Over this work a squared filling on the straight using peacock blue no. 642, tied down with biscuit brown no. 766. The leaf is outlined with heavy chain stitch in two strands of peacock blue no. 644.

2. Left and right middle leaves Work these two leaves in chain stitch in peacock blue nos. 641, 642 and 643.

3. Middle leaf This leaf is worked in battlemented couching, working from dark to light in biscuit brown nos. 763, 765 and 766. The final set of laid threads are tied down with peacock blue no. 643 and the leaf is outlined in stem stitch in peacock blue no. 644.

4. Mounds The mounds are worked in chain stitch as follows:
- Left-hand mound in peacock blue nos. 642 and 643.
- Centre back mound in peacock blue nos. 641 and 642.
- Right-hand mound as left-hand mound.

5. Tree trunk Work the tree trunk in stem stitch in biscuit brown no. 766 for the left and right sides and biscuit brown no 765 for the rest of the trunk.

6. Centre front mound This mound is worked in chain stitch in peacock blue nos. 643 and 644.

7. **Lower leaves of the tree** Work these two leaves in long and short stitch over split stitch in peacock blue nos. 641, 642, 643 and 644.

8. **Rabbit** The rabbit is worked in long and short stitch, working from the nose to the tail and down the legs, using biscuit brown no. 764. The ears are also worked in long and short stitch, in biscuit brown no.764 on the outside and biscuit brown no. 761 on the inside. We want to create the impression of a soft furry coat, so have avoided using split stitch under the long and short stitch.

The eye and nose are worked in two strands of biscuit brown no. 766—with a French knot for the eye and two satin stitches for the nose. The tail is worked in French knots in two strands of biscuit brown no. 761. Stem stitch in biscuit brown no. 766 accentuates the thigh bone of the back leg and some shadow around the front legs.

9. **Squirrel** Like the rabbit, the squirrel is worked in long and short stitch, avoiding the use of split stitch when embroidering the fur.

Work the tail in biscuit brown nos. 763, 764, 765 and 766, working from the end of the tail toward the squirrel's body and from the upper side of the tail to the underside.

The squirrel's body and head are worked in long and short stitch from the back of the animal to the front, using biscuit brown nos. 766 and 764. Biscuit brown no. 766 is used to emphasise the thigh bone and to shade under the front leg.

The ears are worked in straight stitches in biscuit brown no. 764. Two strands of biscuit brown no. 766 are used in a French knot for the eye and in satin stitch for the nut held in the squirrel's paws.

This embroidery is now ready for blocking and making up.

CREATING A TREE OF LIFE DESIGN

It is not necessary to be an artist to be able to sketch out a design for crewel embroidery. What's more, any embroiderer, having once embarked on creating their own small designs, will find it so pleasing that they will not wish to return to working on a design drawn by someone else. The only tools needed are a soft pencil, an eraser and some paper.

Many of the shapes that were popular in crewel embroidery in Jacobean times are still popular today. Because we no longer embroider bed hangings, except in the course of restoration work, today's designs are usually smaller and have often been refined but the Jacobean character, with different flowers and leaves appearing on the same plant, remains.

Designing is not a process which may be rushed—rather it should be carefully worked on until the desired effect is achieved.

The first step is to determine the shape into which your design must fit. Imagine that you are planning to make a rectangular cushion, in which case the overall design will also be rectangular. Neither a square nor a circular design would fit correctly into a rectangular shape.

Having determined the shape and size of your finished piece, the next step is to draw up the shape on paper. You must then decide on the theme of your design. Let us suppose that it will be a Tree of Life design with mounds at the base. The mounds often number three or five, but may be any number. A suggested height for the mounds is about one-fifth the total height of the worked area. If the trunk is to be heavy, the mounds might also be heavy to balance the weight of the trunk. If, on the other hand, the trunk is to be light or more of a stem, you might have a single mound, or a falling leaf crossing the base of the stem, or you might replace the mound with some roots, as though the plant had just been plucked from the ground, roots and all.

The next task is to determine the shape of the trunk and branches or, if the design is delicate, the stems. A study of crewel work designs shows that stems and trunks are usually curved, sometimes gently but at other times quite strongly. The shapes that come to mind are the letters S and C. These letter shapes are recognisable over and over again in crewel work designs.

Begin with the main trunk, letting it widen out at the base as most trees do to give it the appearance of rising quite naturally from the mounds (diagram 1).

I.

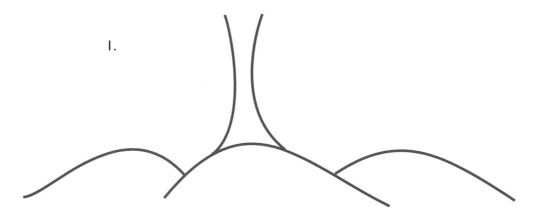

The next step is to venture into branches, perhaps three main branches, making them blend gently into the trunk and letting them fall out towards the sides of the rectangle. If you were designing a wall hanging, which was to be taller than it was wide, the branches might point upwards rather than fall outwards. Take time over this process until a satisfactory outline to your tree has been achieved (diagram 2).

2.

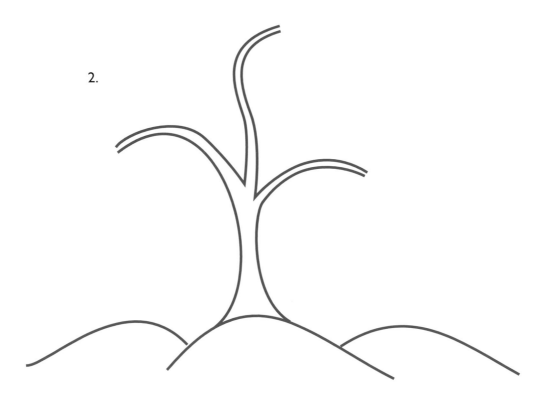

3.

If three branches are insufficient, two more may be added (diagram 3).

Now you can add the flowers and the leaves, arranging them in a balanced way over the tree. The design sheets on pages 87–92 are intended to help you with this process and may be enlarged or reduced as necessary. Alternatively, you might prefer to draw your own flowers and leaves. It is important to attach flowers and leaves at an angle that suggests natural growth. Branches may be shortened or lengthened, or their curves altered as required (diagram 4).

Take time to assess what you have done so far. Check that there is a focal point somewhere just off-centre, that the flowers and leaves are growing from the branches at realistic angles and that they are in the correct proportions. The design should not be too crowded, nor should it be too sparse.

Positioning a leaf across the trunk can give the design a focal point. To fill the gap around the lower left-hand flower you can insert a couple of leaves and a tendril; you can insert another tendril or leaf coming from the lower right-hand branch.

Tufts of grass may be used to add interest to the mounds (diagram 5). Alternatively, small flowers or animals may be added. Note that the last design sheet on page 92 features animals.

4.

5.

DESIGN NO. 10

T he Tree of Life design exercise has been enlarged to produce this design.

Any of the designs in this book may be enlarged before transferring to fabric. It is worth bearing in mind that when a design is enlarged by photocopying, not only are the flowers and leaves enlarged but so also are the stems and trunk, which sometimes results in stems and trunk looking too heavy. This may be rectified by redrawing and refining the stems and trunk before you transfer the design to the fabric.

Two new stitches are encountered in the working of this design, fishbone stitch and bullion knots.

Requirements
Linen twill or fabric of your choice,
    measuring approx. 33 x 38 cm (13 x 15 inches)
Embroidery frame
Crewel needles nos. 3 and 4
Tapestry needle no. 22
Appleton crewel wools (one skein each):
    bright terra cotta nos. 222 and 224
    dull marine blue nos. 321, 323 and 325
    grey-green nos. 353, 354 and 355
    honeysuckle yellow no. 693
    (or crewel wools of your choice)

Method of working
Apply the design and mount the fabric in your frame, making sure that it is very tight.

Work with one thread in the needle unless the instructions indicate otherwise. Refer to the Stitch Glossary for stitch directions.

In working this design, follow the principle adhered to in earlier designs of working the areas in the background before working the areas in the foreground.

1. Stems and trunk These are worked in stem stitch in grey-green nos. 353, 354 and 355. In the case of the stem on the left, the two attached leaves emerge from the back of the stem and should be worked before the stem, using closed fly stitch in grey-green no. 353 for the upper leaf and

grey-green no. 354 for the lower leaf. At this stage work the tendril in stem stitch in grey-green no. 353.

Working clockwise, start with the blue flower on the left:

2. Left-hand blue flower The centre is worked in long and short stitch over split stitch in dull marine blue nos. 321, 323 and 325. The next two petals are worked in battlemented couching using bright terra cotta nos. 222 and 224, tied with dull marine blue no. 323 and outlined in stem stitch in dull marine blue no. 325. The outer petals are worked in fishbone stitch in dull marine blue no. 323.

3. Upper red flower Work the base of this flower in satin stitch over split stitch in grey-green no. 355. The petals are worked in bright terra cotta nos. 222 and 224 in chain stitch, with the stamens in bullion knots worked in honeysuckle yellow no. 693.

4. Top leaves These leaves are each worked in two tones of grey-green in satin stitch over split stitch. For the two upper leaves use nos. 353 and 354, and for the lower leaf use nos. 354 and 355.

5. Right-hand blue flower Work this flower in long and short stitch in dull marine blue nos. 321, 323 and 325 with French knots in two strands of grey-green no. 355.

6. Lower red flower Begin with the leaf which emerges from behind the flower. Work this leaf in closed fly stitch in grey-green no. 355. Continue with the blue petals outlined with two rows of stem stitch in dull marine blue nos. 321 and 323, with seeding in dull marine blue no. 323. The outer petals are worked in fishbone stitch in bright terra cotta no. 224.

7. Middle leaf The centre of this leaf is worked in long and short stitch over split stitch in grey-green nos. 353, 354 and 355, with the vein worked in stem stitch in honeysuckle yellow no. 693. The leaf is outlined in coral stitch worked in two strands of grey-green no. 355.

8. Left and right mounds Begin by working the tufts of grass growing out of these mounds, using long and short stitch over split stitch in honeysuckle yellow no. 693 and grey-green no. 354 as illustrated. The square fillings are worked next, using honeysuckle yellow no. 693, tied with cross-stitches in grey-green no. 354 and French knots worked in two strands of bright terra cotta no. 224. These mounds are outlined in heavy chain stitch in two strands of grey-green no. 354.

9. Central mound This mound is worked in long and short stitch over split stitch in grey-green nos. 353, 354 and 355, leaving space for the tuft of grass in long and short stitch in honeysuckle yellow no. 693.

This embroidery is now ready for blocking and making up.

CREATING A SCROLL DESIGN

If you favour a scroll design for your embroidery, the approach is just as simple as the Tree of Life design.

Cut a paper pattern to the shape of your finished article and draw on it a series of circles. The circles may be similar in size or of differing sizes. In this example there are six circles, but the number of circles you choose will depend on the shape and size of your finished piece of work. Six circles will fit neatly into a rectangle, four or nine will fit into a square. A circular design may be drawn by arranging five circles in a ring around a central circle.

Instead of drawing the circles directly onto the paper pattern, you may prefer to cut a set of paper circles to use as templates. Arrange the circles on the paper pattern, making sure that you leave space between them (diagram 1).

Having arranged the circles to your satisfaction, the next step is to join them, beginning with the pair in the centre. Join them with a letter S, which may be either a forwards S or a backwards S. Sketch lightly so that any lines that don't please you may be erased (diagram 2).

Now extend the head and tail of your S to take in the adjacent circles. Note that you are only ever using part of each of your original circles (diagram 3).

At this point you have used four of the six circles. Now take stems off your S shape to travel part way around the remaining two circles. Your basic scrolls are now complete and you can erase any segments of the circles that are no longer needed (diagram 4).

The final step is to add flowers and leaves to the scrolls, beginning with the focal point, which will be towards the centre of the design. The finished pattern appears as design no. 11.

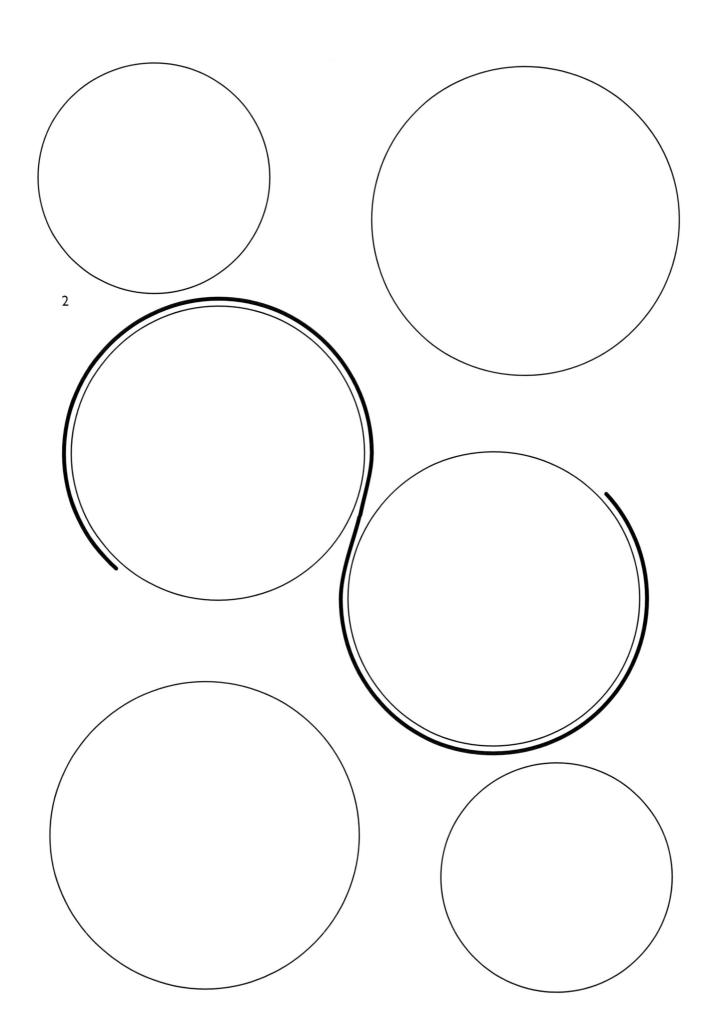

2

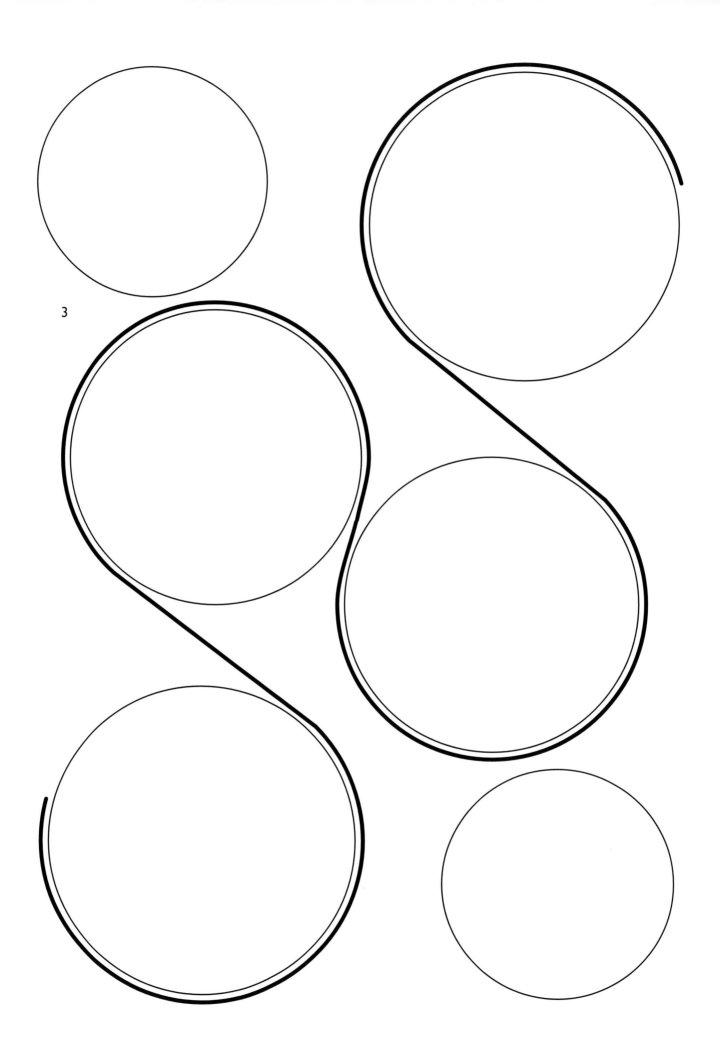

3

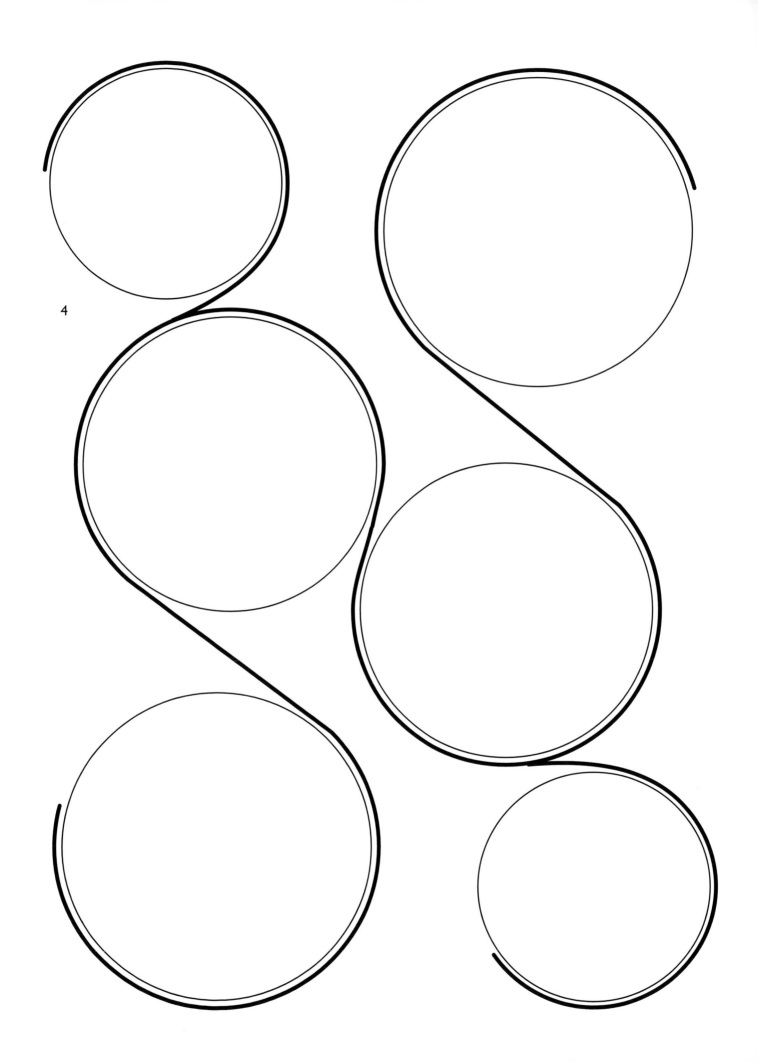

4

DESIGN NO. 11

This design is based on the preceding exercise. Because there are no thick stems, this design lends itself to enlargement by photocopying, which makes it ideal for a larger project.

Requirements

Linen twill or fabric of your choice,
*   measuring approx. 50 x 40 cm (20 x 16 inches)*
Square or rectangular embroidery frame
Crewel needles nos. 3 and 4
Tapestry needle no. 22
Appleton crewel wools (one skein each):
*   flame red nos. 203, 204, 206, 205 and 208*
*   peacock blue nos. 641, 642 and 643*
*   honeysuckle yellow nos. 692, 693 and 694*
*   Jacobean green nos. 291A and 291*
*   (or crewel wools of your choice)*

Method of working

Apply the design and mount the fabric in your frame, making sure that it is very tight.

Work with one thread in the needle, unless instructions indicate otherwise. Refer to the Stitch Glossary for stitch directions.

1. Stems and tendrils The stems are worked in three rows of stem stitch. Jacobean green no. 292 is used on the outside of the stems and no. 291A in the centre. The tendrils are worked in stem stitch in Jacobean green no. 292 and the thorns are worked in long and short stitch in Jacobean green no. 292.

The rest of the design may be worked in the order preferred by the embroiderer. For the purposes of description the central flower is described first, followed by the rest of the leaves and flowers, beginning with the yellow and green leaf and working clockwise around the design.

2. Centre flower The petals of this flower are worked in long and short stitch over split stitch in flame red nos. 203, 204 and 205, starting with the lightest value on the outside and finishing with the darkest tone on the inside. The centre of the flower is worked in a squared filling with threads

laid vertically and horizontally in peacock blue no. 643 and overlaid with diagonal threads in flame red no. 205. The diagonal threads are tied down with an upright cross stitch in flame red no. 208. The flower centre is outlined with stem stitch in flame red no. 208.

3. Yellow and blue leaf This leaf is worked in long and short stitch over split stitch, beginning at the tip of the leaf with honeysuckle yellow no. 693, followed by honeysuckle yellow no. 694 then progressing to peacock blue nos. 642 and 643.

4. Sprig of small leaves Here the stem is worked in stem stitch in Jacobean green no. 292. Work the small leaves in closed fly stitch, embroidering the upper four leaves in Jacobean green no. 291A and the remaining three leaves in Jacobean green no. 292.

5. Leaf with curled edge Begin this leaf with a squared filling, laying horizontal and vertical threads in flame red no. 206 tied down with peacock blue no. 642. Add French knots in peacock blue no. 642. Work the outline to this section of the leaf with stem stitch in peacock blue no. 642.

The curled edge of the leaf is worked in long and short stitch over split stitch in peacock blue nos. 641, 642 and 643, beginning at the point of the leaf.

6. Small yellow buds The stem is worked in stem stitch in Jacobean green no 292 and the buds are worked in stem stitch in honeysuckle yellow, no. 693 on the outside and no. 694 inside.

7. Red and blue flower Begin this flower with the centre petal, working the outline in two rows of stem stitch in flame red no. 206 on the outside and no. 205 on the inside. The centre of the petal is worked in stem stitch and detached chain stitch in peacock blue no. 642.

The next pair of petals are worked in long and short stitch over split stitch, using one row of flame red no. 204, around the outer edge, followed by one row of no. 205, with the remaining area being filled in with one or two rows of no. 206, as required. Work the left-hand petal first because that is behind the right-hand petal.

Finally, work the lower petals in long and short stitch over split stitch in peacock blue nos. 641 and 642.

8. Small green and red leaf This leaf is worked in long and short stitch in Jacobean green nos. 292 and 291 and flame red no. 204.

9. Narrow leaf Work this leaf in fishbone stitch in Jacobean green no. 291.

10. Yellow daisy The daisy petals are worked in rows of chain stitch in honeysuckle gold nos. 692, 693 and 694, finishing with flame red no. 205 in the centre of each petal. The outer petals are worked first, then the next pair of petals and finally the centre petal. The centre of the daisy is worked in French knots in Jacobean green nos. 291A and 291.

11. Red and blue leaf The leaf is worked in battlemented couching in flame red nos. 204, 206 and 208, working from dark to light. The last set of laid stitches is tied down with peacock blue no 643. French knots are added in honeysuckle gold no. 694. The outline is worked in two rows of stem stitch in peacock blue no. 643 on the outside and no. 642 inside.

12. Larger green and red leaf Work this leaf in long and short stitch over split stitch using Jacobean green no. 291 on the outside, followed by Jacobean green no. 291A and flame red no. 204.

13. Yellow and green flower Begin with the back of the flower, working long and short stitch over split stitch in honeysuckle yellow nos. 693 and 694. Now work the stamens in stem stitch in Jacobean green no. 291 and work a French knot in two strands of flame red no. 205 on the end of each stamen.

Next work the front of the flower in long and short stitch over split stitch, beginning at the top edge with honeysuckle yellow no. 692 followed by Jacobean green no. 291A. The remaining area is filled in with long and short stitch in Jacobean green no. 291. The calyx is worked in closed fly stitch in Jacobean green no. 292.

14. Two red buds Work these two buds in long and short stitch over split stitch in flame red nos. 204 and 205, with the calyx in Jacobean green no. 292.

15. Large blue leaf This leaf is worked in long and short stitch over split stitch in peacock blue nos. 641, 642 and 643. The vein of the leaf is worked in stem stitch in flame red no. 206.

16. Small red and green leaf Work this leaf with a squared filling, laying stitches horizontally and vertically using Jacobean green no. 291 and then laying diagonal stitches in flame red no. 204 tied down with straight crosses in flame red no. 206.

This embroidery is now ready for blocking and making up.

This scroll design is the final project. Although colours and stitches have been specified for each of the projects in this book, embroiderers are encouraged to use their own taste in colour and to experiment with different stitches. Do remember, however, that it is essential to retain the shading which gives crewel work its character.

BLOCKING

Once the embroidery is complete, the work is ready for blocking. This is not a difficult process once you have gathered together the necessary equipment:

- A piece of board larger than the piece of fabric you are blocking. Chipboard works well.
- Cotton fabric for covering the board. Old sheeting is good for this purpose.
- Drawing pins, tacks or nails.
- A hammer.
- A spray bottle for spraying the back of the work with water.

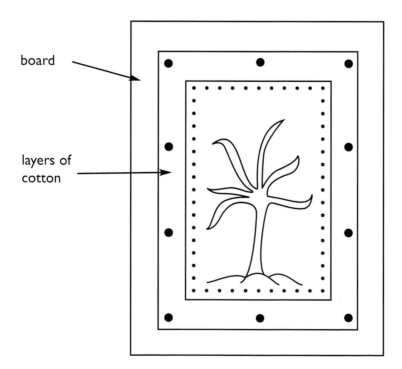

Cover the board with three layers of cotton, secured at each corner and every 20 cm (8 inches) along each side with drawing pins, tacks or nails.

Position the embroidery, face down, on the blocking board and pin the top edge at 2 cm (¾ inch) intervals.

Now pin one of the vertical sides in the same way, making sure that the top and side are at right angles to each other.

Pin the third and fourth sides in the same way, once again making sure that the corners form right angles.

Once the work is pinned out satisfactorily, spray the back of it thoroughly with water and leave it in a horizontal position to dry out naturally. This may take one to two days, depending on the weather.

When the work is thoroughly dry, remove the pinning and make up as desired. Making up should follow immediately after blocking.

DESIGN SHEETS

These design sheets provide a source of flowers, leaves, animals and other motifs suitable for use in crewel designs. These motifs may be copied, enlarged or reduced as needed to match the scale of a particular design.

Only the outlines are presented as these shapes may be worked in any way the embroiderer wishes. The stitches and their arrangement may be simple or complex.

Such motifs are the greatest friend to the embroiderer who is nervous when it comes to designing. No two people will use them in the same way, so every embroiderer will produce an original design.

STITCH GLOSSARY

Bullion knot

Bullion knots, once mastered, are quick to work and have many applications.

To begin, bring the needle up at A and take it down at B, leaving a loop of thread on the surface of the fabric. Bring the needle part the way up again at A and wrap the loop of thread round the needle for a distance equal to the space between A and B.

Once there are sufficient wraps on the needle, hold them in place with the thumb and forefinger of the left hand while gently drawing the needle through with the right hand. The needle is now taken down at B and the thread is tightened as required.

If the wraps of thread appear uneven, the needle may be used to stroke them into place on the underside of the knot.

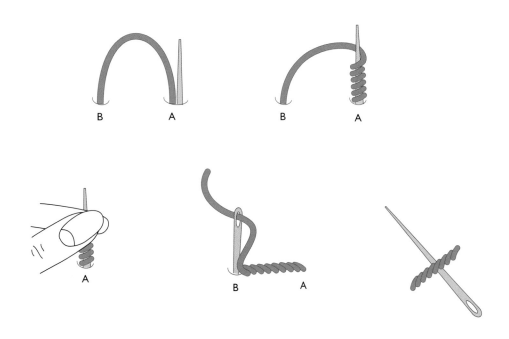

Buttonhole stitch

Buttonhole stitch is a very versatile stitch with many variations. Here we are looking at spaced buttonhole stitch.

Bring the needle up at A, take it down at B and bring it up at C. Now tighten the thread to the desired tension. Continue the line of stitches in this way, keeping the spaces even.

Chain stitch

Chain stitch is a very useful stitch with many applications. It may be used to create a line or worked in close rows to form a filling, in which case the rows must all be worked in the same direction. Alternatively, a chain stitch may be stitched singly, in which case it is known as detached chain stitch.

To begin, bring the needle up at A and take it down in the same spot, leaving a loop of thread on the surface of the fabric. Bring the needle up at B, inside the loop. Gently draw the thread through the loop until the desired tension is achieved. To make the second stitch, take the needle down at B and bring it up at C, inside the loop. The line of stitching continues in this way. To finish the line of stitching, bring the thread out at B on the final stitch and take the needle down outside the loop.

To work chain stitch around an angle in a design, such as the point of a leaf, complete a line of chain stitch along one side of the leaf, taking the needle to the back of the work after the last chain. Anchor the thread on the back of the work by taking a small stitch where it will not be seen. Now bring the needle up at the point of the leaf, ready to continue stitching along the remaining side.

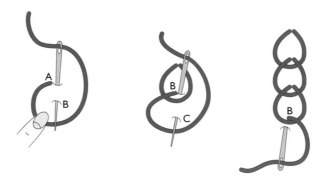

Chain stitch, detached

To make a detached chain stitch, bring the needle up at A and take it down at A, holding a loop of thread on the surface of the work. Bring the needle up at B and draw the thread through as though making a line of chain stitches. Finally, secure the detached chain stitch by taking the needle down at C.

Chain stitch, heavy

Heavy chain makes a very distinct line and is suitable for outlining a shape containing an open filling. Once mastered, this stitch quickly becomes a favourite.

A tapestry needle is the best tool for this stitch to ensure that neither the ground fabric nor the working thread is pierced by the needle.

To work heavy chain stitch, begin with a detached chain stitch as already described, bringing the needle up at A and down in the same spot, coming up at B and going down at C. Now bring the needle up a short distance below C at D, take it under the chain already made and down again at D.

Bring the needle up a short distance below D at E. Now take it under the last chain and under the tie-down stitch B–C, and down at E.

Continue by bringing the needle up at F and passing it under the previous two chains to go down again at F.

The line of stitching continues in this way, always bringing the needle up below the last completed stitch and passing it under the previous two chains. The tension is firm but not tight.

Coral stitch

Coral stitch, also called coral knot, creates a textured line. The knots may be close together or spaced out, depending on the desired effect. Coral stitch may be used as a line stitch or in shaded rows as a filling. When coral stitch is worked in two or more rows, the knots of each successive row are spaced between the knots of the previous row.

Working from right to left, bring the needle up at A and lay the thread down along the stitching line to the left of A. Take the needle down at B and bring it up at C inside the loop made by the thread. Note that the stitch B–C is made at right angles to the stitching line. Gently draw the thread up at right angles to the fabric and then lay it down along the stitching line ready to make the next stitch.

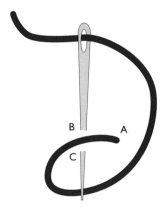

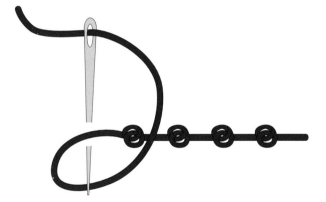

Fishbone stitch

Fishbone stitch is used to form a solid filling suitable for leaf shapes. Draw a guideline along the centre of the shape. Begin stitching by bringing the needle up at the point of the shape, A, and taking it down at B. Bring the needle up at C to the left of A and take it down at D to the right of B.

Next bring the needle up at E to the right of A and take it down at F to the left of B. Continue in this way, bringing the needle up on alternate sides along the edge of the shape and taking it down on the opposite side, just beyond the centre line, until the shape is filled.

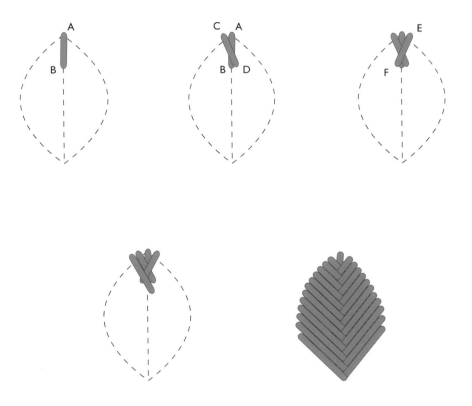

Fly stitch

Fly stitch may be worked either as an open filling or a solid filling.

To work fly stitch, bring the needle up at A, take it down at B and bring it up again at C, inside the loop formed by A–B. To complete the stitch, take the needle over the loop A–B and down at D. This stitch may be used as a scattered filling.

An open filling may be created by working fly stitches in a vertical line.

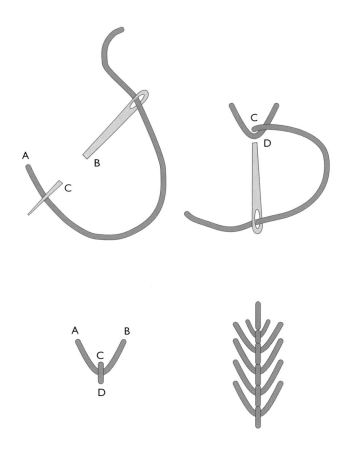

Fly stitch, closed

To make a solid filling, closed fly stitch is used. The closed fly stitch uses a much shorter tie-down stitch than the open fly stitch.

To fill a leaf with closed fly stitch, begin at the tip of the leaf with a straight stitch, bring the needle up at A and take it down at B at least 6 mm (¼ inch) away. Bring the needle up at C, close to and to the left of A. Take the needle down at D, to the right of A, and bring it up at B, inside the loop formed by C–D. Take it down at E, ready to begin the next stitch. Continue in this way, following the outline of the shape. Although the tie-down stitches are short, they need to be long enough to maintain a good slope on the 'wings' of the fly stitch. If the tie-down stitches become too short, the characteristic slope of the 'wings' will be lost.

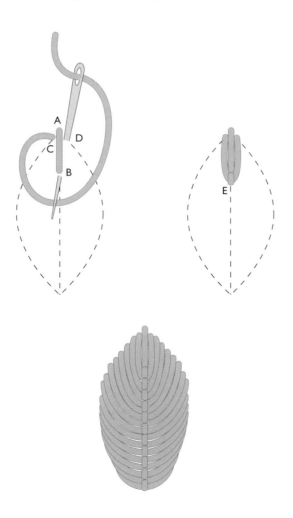

French knots

French knots seem to work best when a double thread is used.

To begin a French knot, bring the needle up at A. Placing the needle in front of the emerging thread, take the thread once round the needle and insert the needle into the fabric close to but not into A. Gently tension the working thread, sliding the knot down the needle until it sits on the fabric. Now draw the needle and thread through the fabric to produce a neat knot.

French knots may be worked closely to form a line or scattered at random to form a light filling. They may also be worked in close rows when a solid filling is required.

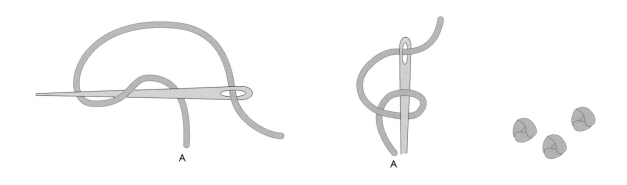

Herringbone stitch

Herringbone stitch may be worked as a light and open filling or worked closely to give a dense filling. The illustration shows an open stitch.

Working from left to right, commence the herringbone stitch by bringing the needle up at A, going down at B and coming up at C. Take the needle down at D and come up again at E. Continue in this way until the line of stitching is complete.

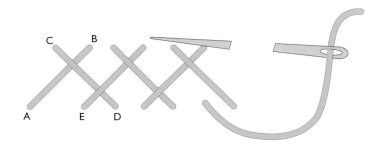

Herringbone stitch, threaded

To work threaded herringbone stitch, begin by working a row of herringbone stitch as already illustrated. Using a tapestry needle threaded with a contrasting colour, work the new thread over and under the stitches already worked, as shown in the illustration. Note that the new thread only enters the fabric at the start and finish of the line of stitching.

Herringbone stitch, tied

Tied herringbone stitch is another variation on the basic stitch. Begin by working a row of herringbone stitch and then tie the herringbone stitches with a vertical straight stitch, using the same or a contrasting colour. In this stitch the ties enter the fabric with each stitch.

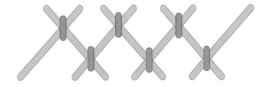

Laid work

Laid stitches are worked backwards and forwards across a shape without carrying the thread across the back of the shape. The stitches lie parallel to each other and close together, as in satin stitch. Begin the laid stitches in the centre of the shape, working first in one direction and then returning to the centre and working in the opposite direction.

To lay the stitches, bring the thread up at A and take it down at B. The next stitch comes up at C next to B and goes down at D next to A. To make the third stitch, bring the needle up at E and take it down at F. Continue in this way to fill the area.

Once the laid stitches are completed, they need to be couched down. Couching may be worked in a variety of ways. The illustrations show fly stitch, back stitch and a squared filling used as couching stitches. Either a matching thread or a contrasting colour may be used.

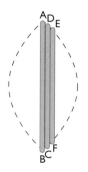 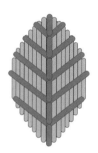  

Long and short stitch

The phrase 'long and short stitch' makes many an otherwise experienced embroiderer quake, yet once mastered it becomes an invaluable part of the stitch repertoire. Only the stitches in the first row are worked alternately long and short. All stitches in subsequent rows are of similar length.

There must be a clear distinction between the long stitches and the short stitches in the first row or the whole effect will be lost. Make the short stitches about two-thirds the length of the long stitches.

If you have not previously worked long and short stitch, you may find it easier if you practise it across a horizontal line, rather than trying to work around a leaf or a petal shape.

To begin, work a row of split stitch in the colour that you will use for your first row of long and short stitch. Although the split stitch will be covered it is still important to work it with care. Any weakness in the split stitch will spoil your long and short stitches.

Row 1

Once the split stitch is completed, proceed with the first row of long and short stitch, bringing the needle up at A and taking it down over the edge of the split stitch at B. Bring the needle up at C and take it down at D outside the split stitch. Make a row of stitches alternately long and short, with the long stitches being 12–18 mm (½–¾ inch) long and the short stitches about two-thirds the length of the long stitches.

Row 2

Work the second row in the opposite direction, with the needle coming up and splitting the first row of stitches about one-quarter of the way back into the stitches.

Begin this second row by bringing the needle up at F and taking it down at G. Come up at H and go down at I. All stitches in the second and subsequent rows will be long stitches, although they will not necessarily be identical in length.

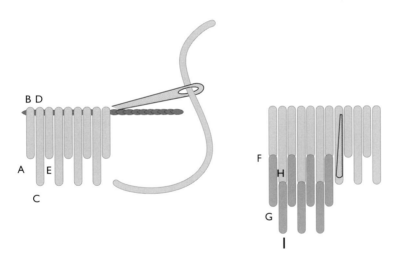

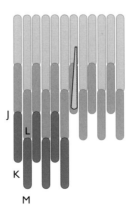

Row 3

The third row of long and short stitch is worked in the same direction as the second, bringing the needle up at J and taking it down at K, then bringing it up at L and taking it down at M.

The working of long and short stitches in straight rows, as described above, is called tapestry shading. It is worth becoming familiar with tapestry shading before going on to apply long and short stitch to leaf and petal shapes.

Leaves and petals

When working a leaf in long and short stitch, first work split stitch round the edge of the shape and then mark in the directional lines for the stitches, using a hard pencil or a water-erasable pen. Begin the first row of long and short stitch at the point of the leaf, bringing the needle up within the leaf shape at A and taking it down over the edge of the split stitch at B. Work down one side of the leaf before stitching down the other side. Insert half stitches on the edge as necessary to make the long and short stitches align with the directional lines.

Once the first row of long and short stitch has been worked, proceed with the next row using the next colour value. As with tapestry shading, the stitches in the second and subsequent rows are long stitches. Varying the length of the stitches will give the effect of gentle shading. If the space to be filled diminishes, as is usually the case, stitches can be left out to suit the space available.

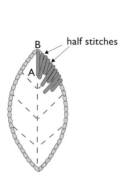

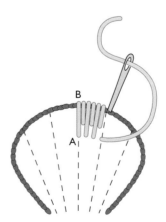

When embroidering a petal, first work a row of split stitch around the edge of the petal and then mark in the directional lines for the placement of the long and short stitches. Begin the first row of long and short stitches at the centre of the petal, coming up within the shape at A and going down over the edge of the split stitch at B. Work one side of the petal, return to the centre of the petal and work the opposite side. When a directional line is reached, a long or short stitch should lie parallel with that line. Use half stitches as necessary to make the stitches align with the directional lines.

Long and short stitches need to be sufficiently close to prevent fabric showing between them but not so close that they cramp each other.

Satin stitch

A row of split stitch worked round the edge of a shape before working the satin stitch will give a good clean line to the shape.

As a general rule, begin the satin stitch in the centre of the shape and work to one side, then return to the centre and work to the opposite side. Satin stitch may be worked straight or slanting. Beware of finishing a narrow shape with a very small stitch which would make it difficult to achieve a neat appearance.

Bring the needle up at A on one side of the shape and take it down at B on the opposite side of the shape. To make the next stitch bring the needle up at C, next to A, and take it down next to B. Continue in this way until one-half of the shape is stitched and then return to the centre to commence stitching the second half.

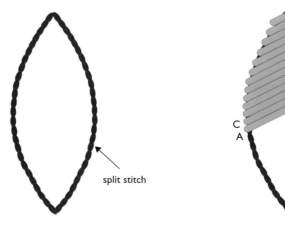

split stitch

Seeding

Seeding is a very useful stitch for crewel embroidery when a light filling is required. The stitches are basically back stitches worked in different directions within a shape. The stitches may be close together or spaced out. They may be worked in one colour value or shaded with two or three values of the one colour.

Seeding stitches may be worked singly, or in pairs with two stitches emerging from the same spot but lying at a slight angle to each other.

Split stitch

Split stitch is very similar to stem stitch, except that the needle comes up splitting the working thread rather than emerging to one side as it does when working stem stitch.

This is a stitch which is used very frequently, as a padding under satin stitch or long and short stitch. It may also be used as a line stitch or as a filling, in which case the rows must all be stitched in the same direction.

Working from left to right, bring the needle up at A, take it down at B and bring it up again at C, splitting the stitch already made. C is halfway between A and B. Continue in this way, always splitting the previous stitch.

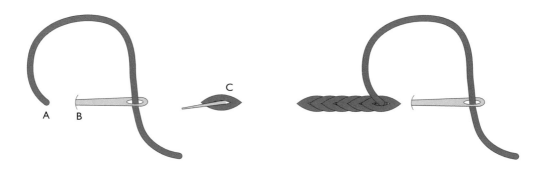

Squared fillings

Squared fillings are very useful in crewel embroidery. They cover an area quickly and, depending on the spacing of the threads and the depth of colouring, may be light or heavy.

Beginning at the widest section of the shape, lay single threads across the shape, first in one direction and then in the opposite direction.

Commence with a few running stitches along the edge of the shape and come up at A for the first stitch. Take the needle down at B and bring it up at C, next to B. Go down at D, on the opposite side and next to A, to complete the second stitch. Come up at E and go down at F for the third stitch. Continue in this way until one-half of the shape is filled, then go back to the centre of the shape and work in the other direction.

To assist in keeping the stitches parallel to each other, cut a piece of lightweight card to a width equal to the distance you require between the lines. Use the card as a guide when inserting the needle.

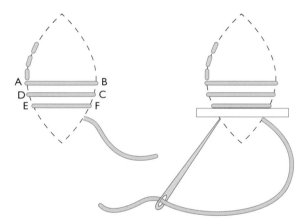

Once the stitches are laid in each direction, the intersections can be tied down with a cross-stitch or a half cross-stitch. This forms the simplest of the squared fillings. The fillings may be further enhanced with a French knot in the centre of each square.

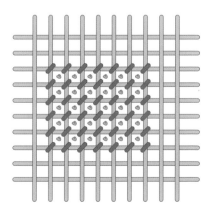

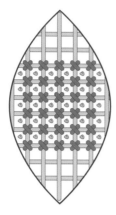 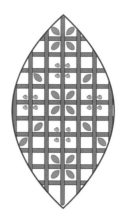 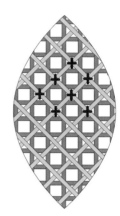

Instead of French knots, detached chain stitches may be placed inside the squares, or a combination of detached chain stitches and French knots may be used.

Another type of squared filling is laid out with horizontal and vertical stitches and then overlaid with stitches on the diagonal. The diagonal stitches may then be tied down with a straight stitch or a cross-stitch.

Battlemented couching

Battlemented couching is one of the square fillings much favoured by crewel embroiderers.

A grid of vertical and horizontal lines is shaded from light to dark or dark to light.

Begin by working a basic squared filling with horizontal and vertical threads. The illustrated example has the basic filling worked in the darkest shade. Over these threads and to the side of them, lay a second set of threads in the next value of the chosen colour. Continue in this way with the third and, if required, the fourth set of threads. There is no rule about

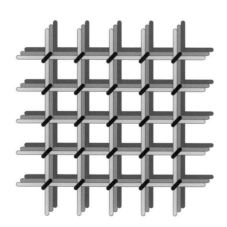

whether the horizontal or the vertical thread should be worked first, but the first set of threads determines the order for the subsequent sets.

When all the threads are laid, the final horizontal and vertical threads are tied down with a half cross-stitch in a contrasting thread. If space permits, a French knot may be added inside each of the squares.

Stem stitch

Stem stitch is one of the most frequently used stitches in crewel embroidery, forming a fine line with a single row of stitching, a broad line with several rows or a solid filling with multiple shaded rows worked within a shape.

Work stem stitch from left to right, bringing the needle up at A, taking it down at B and bringing it up at C, before tightening the stitch and keeping the working thread below the needle. This will result in a thicker line than if the thread is kept above the needle, and the stitches will be more clearly defined.

On the other hand, keeping the working thread above the needle will result in a fine line with the stitches blending into each other. Try both methods and take note of the different effects which result.

Once a line of stem stitch is begun, the thread must continue to be kept on the same side of the needle.

When working a curved stem or shape, stem stitch makes a smoother line if the thread is held towards the outside of the curve.

When working several rows of stem stitch for a broad stem, work all rows in the same direction until you come to the final row. Stitch the final row in the opposite direction with the thread on the opposite side.

If stem stitch is worked round a sharp curve, the stitches will need to be shortened in order to make a smooth line.

When using stem stitch as a filling, each row must be worked in the same direction.

To connect a branch to a main stem or trunk, work the main stem first and then work the branch from the outer tip back towards the main stem, continuing to work a few stitches along the side of the main stem.

Straight stitch

This is the easiest stitch to make, simply bringing the needle up at A and taking it down at B. We have already met it in such stitches as detached chain stitch, satin stitch, long and short stitch, seeding and so on.

Worked as a single stitch, straight stitch is used to depict a blade of grass or, when worked in a group of three or more, a tuft of grass, as shown in the illustration. The needle comes up at A and goes down at B, up at C and down again at B and finally up at D and down at B.

Groups of straight stitches may be worked one below another to form a vertical line or side by side to form a horizontal line.

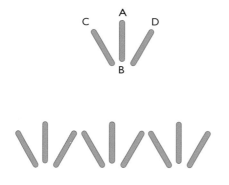

ABOUT THE AUTHOR

Shelagh Amor grew up in England, where she pursued a career in accounting before marrying and settling in Australia.

Although she had taken up a needle at an early age, it wasn't until after the birth of her second child that she discovered the Embroiderers' Guild and, through it, the many facets of the art of embroidery.

For Shelagh, embroidery became a passion, first patchwork then counted thread techniques — canvaswork, pulled thread, Hardanger, and blackwork — and, with time, she developed skills in crewel embroidery. She passed on her skills by conducting regular classes covering all of these techniques, and became widely known for her gift for spreading her enthusiasm for embroidery.

Shelagh used her administrative skills to co-ordinate classes for the Embroiderers' Guild and to promote embroidery in her local community. From 1984 to 1986 she served as President of the Embroiderers' Guild, Victoria.

In twenty years of teaching, Shelagh has established a reputation for her meticulous attention to detail and finish. She now finds that it is crewel embroidery which most captures her imagination, from the first pencil line on paper to the last stitch on the linen.

Shelagh Amor currently teaches crewel embroidery at all levels, both in the classroom and by correspondence. She sees it as her mission in life to make the time honoured technique of crewel embroidery as enjoyable as possible for her students.

ACKNOWLEDGEMENTS

My thanks go to the Embroiderers' Guild, Victoria, where I began my pursuit of crewel embroidery, and especially to its co-founder Morna Sturrock, who never fails to support and encourage all embroiderers.

I also thank everyone associated with Sally Milner Publishing for their support from the very first draft.

Finally, I thank my husband John for his contribution to this project.

SHELAGH AMOR, 2002